Yes! You are a Champion

Turning Everyday Challenges into Victory

Published by Godzchild Publications
a division of Godzchild, Inc.
22 Halleck St., Newark, NJ 07104
www.godzchildproductions.net

Printed in the United States of America 2011 – First Edition Book
Cover designed by Keisha Jacobs.

Library of Congress Cataloging-in-Publications Data
God Created Us Champions/Kellie Thompson.

ISBN 978-1-9370950-5-5 (pbk.)

1. Thompson, Kellie. 2. Inspirational. 3. Christianity.
4. Religion. 5. Encouragement.

2011930056

Table of Contents

Yes! You Are A Champion

Endorsement

Yes! You are a Champion: Turning Everyday Challenges Into Victory is a must have for your library!
Kellie shares life challenges on how to fight the good fight of faith!!! She shows you how to endure the fight as a good soldier … in spite of the many failures you face in life; she encourages you to awaken the champion inside you, as she reminds you of the Word of God "He always causes you to triumph."
Although it may seem like life's storms and adversities have knocked you out, on count number 8 you find yourself still down … it may even seem like you can't get back up before the bell.
Listen to your trainer, Kellie, as she gets into the ring with you … commanding you to get back up … declaring that you can still win in spite of how many times you've been knocked down.
This book does not only encourage adults but young people as well, as she pours out uncompromised truths on how she overcame traumatic situations as a young child through her biblical upbringing.

Patrina Suydam, President / Founder of the Not My Kids Foundation, Inc.

Foreword

You are a Champion! Kellie Thompson does a dynamic job sharing that we were created by God to be Champions. This book can be used as a guide to turn everyday challenges into victory after victory. I have learned that we must be students of God's word in order to be confident. Confidence produces actions and when your actions line up with the Word of God you will have godly results.

I have known Kellie for many years. As a member of Spirit of Faith Christian Center, I have had many opportunities to watch her develop into the woman of God that she is. I am delighted to know that she is in hot pursuit of what God has destined for her to do in order to impact the lives of others. The information provided in this book will help you to be the Champion that God has created you to be.

Dr. Dee Dee Freeman

Chapter 1
Yes, You are a Champion!

> *Struggle is inevitable, but failure has always been optional.*
> *- Kellie Thompson*

How do you win the contest of life? I am glad you asked because this book will teach you how to win and how to remain a champion. Struggles, battles, and storms are inevitable, but failure is optional. The word of God says in 2 Corinthians 2:14 "Now thanks be unto God, which always causeth us to triumph in Christ, and maketh manifest the savor of his knowledge by us in every place."

A champion is one who holds or wins first place in a contest or sport. A champion is also one who fights for, defends, and supports a cause of another person. If life is a contest then you have already won! 2 Corinthians said God causes us to always triumph! That means you have already been declared the winner before the fight! Yes, You are a Champion!

You are called to fight the good fight of faith, to lay hold on eternal life. Therefore, just get on in the ring of life, defend your cause, and establish your fighting strategy as a good fighter is always cognizant of his opponent.

When I was growing up, boxing was my favorite sport. I loved to watch boxing because it was full of surprises; you could not always predict who would win. I recalled watching Mike Tyson knock out Michael Spinks in the first 91 seconds of the fight, thus becoming the undisputed heavyweight champion of the world. No one really expected Mike Tyson to beat Michael Spinks, as this was his first loss in his professional career. Boxing is one of those sports where size does not really matter. Time and time again I have literally seen the shortest, smallest boxer take down an opponent who was both taller and bigger.

You may be asking what this fight has to do with you. Trust and believe when Mike Tyson trained for every fight, he studied and knew everything about his opponent's fighting style. My question to you is who is your opponent? Is it doubt, Is it unbelief? Is it drugs, Is it alcohol? Is it debt? Is it poverty? You must be cognizant of your opponent and know what you are fighting for.

The Bible says in Ephesians 6:12,"For we wrestle not against flesh and blood, but against principalities, against powers, against the rulers of the darkness of this world, against spiritual wickedness in high places." As Champions, you must know at some point in life, you will experience many obstacles or hardships in life.

A boxer goes into the ring knowing that he or she will encounter hard punches during the match, so prepare yourself by staying focused on your goals. It is important because when you are presented with an obstacle, you will be able to stand strong because you are not just fighting; you are fighting with a purpose. You may not win each round, but trust and believe you will win the match. Experience has taught me many lessons such as never focus on the bad situations, always focus on the good, and always remember to have faith in God.

A great boxer does not give up in the first round; he continues to fight until he knocks out his opponent or wins the fight by the judge's decision after all 12 rounds are over. On rare occasions, a fighter's trainer may actually throw a towel in the ring when the fighter receives too many powerful blows from his opponent, but only a focused fighter endures the blows and continues to fight to the end.

In life, you do not have anyone controlling whether or not you will throw in the towel. It is up to you to stay in the fight. You can beat the odds and win the fight! To be the champion, you must possess a strategy. You must be mentally, physically, and emotionally ready for whatever challenge you embark on. The most important strategy is to know that the word of God has already declared you a winner. You must also love yourself. Unfortunately, many believers' fight is within themselves. Because of past failures, you can't forgive yourself, thus feeling unworthy, and defeated. How do you love yourself? YOU MUST SAY IT! Speaking is the first step to any great process.

If someone wants to go to college, he must say to himself "I want to go to college", and then he must take the necessary steps to start college, such as applying, going to visit, and evaluating the programs offered. The same is true with loving yourself; you start by saying, "I love my self, God loves me and has forgiven me. I am a Champion, because God has always caused me to triumph! I am a winner! I will achieve all of my goals."

In addition, loving yourself is not allowing negative thoughts to dominate your life. You must fight mentally in order to love yourself. Your thoughts determine your future. Consider monitoring your thoughts a little closer than you have in the past. Think about the possibilities of winning and stop worrying about the impossibilities. Things may come to discourage you, but do not let the discouragements defeat you.

A Champion is a finisher. I remember when I was a student at Dudley Beauty, we started with a large number of students. However, when we graduated, there were a few graduates out of the many that started. I believe that was a direct result of discouragement, negative thoughts; or unfortunate situations. Some students actually did excellent work but they lacked endurance and dropped out two months before graduation. It was not easy. I got discouraged because I did not have any money. I was in school, so I did not work that often. On my days off, I spent most of my time studying, but would get upset because I wanted to go shopping with my friends even though I could not afford to go shopping.

In life, you do not have anyone controlling whether or not you will throw in the towel just because you have experienced some powerful blows.

Today many individuals are faced with similar adversity. Whatever challenges you are encountering, I encourage you to stay in the fight and finish. Do not give up! Prepare yourself for the next round. You are a Champion!

My parents were my personal trainers, in my corner encouraging me to continue and to finish. I could have begged them to let me throw in the towel and they would have refused. They would always say, "Do not stop; always believe in yourself."

You see, a Champion needs support and love from someone. You may not have your parents in your corner, but you have God. Joshua 1:5 says that God will never leave you nor forsake you. So stand tall and never doubt because God is with you.

You can finish strong because you are a Champion. Even though you might not feel like it right now, you must believe it; keep saying it, "I am a Champion". I am your personal cheerleader. Yes, I am cheering for you! You can do the impossible, and you can reach the sky with God on your side and the Word of God in your heart.

If you pay close attention, you will find out a lot about life. God placed an imagination in all of us. In fact, our experiences are one of our greatest sources of knowledge. Just think about it: we have a mind to learn, we learn to cook by observation, toddlers learn by imitation, students learn through demonstration, we learn to love by inspiration, we learn to strive by motivation, and we learn vision and faith by meditation. Therefore, we should learn something new every day.

Since I was young, I have always been motivated to succeed in life. I always had a desire to be successful. I have never been comfortable with living my life in a box. I have never thought of myself to be average or like everyone else. Although I admire many individuals, I never wanted to be like everyone else.

I have always stated that I want to be the best **Kellie** that I can be. I have always been a self-motivated Champion. No one can teach you what your passion is. However, you can be trained on how to succeed in your passion. My passion in life is to educate others on how to survive powerful blows in life and declare their victory through faith. God can reveal your passion to you and give you the strength and the courage you need to bring that passion to life.

When I graduated from Beauty College, I was anxious

to start my business. I had to be a business owner because I never wanted to experience termination again. It was a terrible feeling that caused me to work hard daily to reach my dream of becoming a successful business owner. What I did not know was that it would take some time to make that dream a reality and build a strong clientele.

The first couple of months were painful. At times, I only made enough money to cover my expenses. Often times I did not make any profit. Not a dollar over! I thought about quitting and looking into another career, but I had to stay persistent and optimistic. Sometimes adversity can serve as a reason to change your mind. It has stopped many people from following their dreams. Your mind is a very powerful tool and it must be used as a motor to keep you going when faced with challenges.

Adversity had me against the ropes saying to me "You are broke and have no clients", but I prayed to God, as my family always did during rough times. I began to see the bright side of the situation and I came out swinging. At least I made enough to cover my expenses. Some would say, "Well that's not Success." Maybe you don't think so, but I looked at it optimistically - I was still in business.

Eventually I started seeing so much profit. I was able to buy my first car. I was so excited because I now had an option to get in my car or to ride the bus or train to work.

Success is having options. I did not allow adversity to take away my focus. I used adversity to help me win the round. I gained great courage and self-confidence in my ability to do absolutely anything I dreamed of doing. Glory to God!

I can recall the first day that I made a thousand dollars in one day; I was so excited because I was having so much fun servicing clients; I didn't even remember collecting that much money. I was actually being paid a lot of money for something I actually love doing. Wow!

As I stated earlier, sometimes adversity can serve as a reason to get you to change your mind. It has stopped many people from following their dreams. When I was counting that money, I remembered the time when I was homeless and living in a hotel. I felt so proud; I was going home to my very own house via my very own car? I had a lot to be proud of that day. I believe that we must celebrate our victories, and that day I did. I was on cloud nine; no one could have told me that when I was homeless that I would experience making that much money one day. I began to cry when counting that money because I could have quit and never experienced that day. Life is funny because in the middle of my storm, I did not think that in the end I would be able to make that much money while having that much fun. Through faith and patience, I saw my dreams in manifestation and I am in full expectancy for greater and greater things happening in my life. Yes! You are a Champion.

Sometimes adversity can serve as a reason to get you to change your mind. It has stopped many people from following their dreams

Therefore, you should look forward to great things happening in your life too. In this book, you can learn from my story of diligence and high self-esteem. I always knew I was destined for greatness. You are also destined for greatness. We really do not know the totality of the greatness in us, so the best thing to do is to stay positive through every situation. Remember, the longer you stay in the fight, the chances of you winning increase.

Dear God,
Thank you for teaching me to be a champion in you. I ask you to help me stay focused in every area of my life. I will become more positive in the way I look at life and its challenges. I ask you to bless me in every dream that I pursue that is in agreement with your plan for my life and to send someone to help me with each step. Now, I thank you for everything that I have prayed for because I believe it is your will for me.
In Jesus' Name I pray, AMEN.

Chapter 2

Homelessness Doesn't Mean Hopelessness

Hope is a tool that gives you a sense of peace when all hell is breaking loose in your life.
- Kellie Thompson

At the age of 16, my family and I were forced from our home. It was so painful because "Home is where the heart is." To not have a home crushed my heart. I asked myself as we put our clothes in our car, "Why me? Why us?" I was enjoying the best times before that; I was on the honor roll; I was happy. Out of nowhere, I am homeless. I could not believe it. The sad part is that it was not my parents fault.

My mom had just been awarded her first government contract, so we were doing pretty well at that time. And then my dad received an unexpected call about taking care of his mother. Of course, without hesitation, the Christian duty would be to bestow due benevolence to the extent of your family member's need. How can you turn your back on the needs of your own mother? My dad was told everything would be willed to him as a result of his choice to care for his mother. Wow! This must be God! My parents made the decision to willingly give up their current home at the time, to become full-time caregivers for my grandmother.

As time went on, while we were caring for my grandmother, another relative surfaced out of nowhere. Things became extremely ugly overnight. People started calling the house threatening to do us bodily harm. The threats came from the anger my aunt had towards my grandmother's decision to choose my dad as her caregiver. Immediately the ridiculing and persecution began. On several occasions, my aunt had all of our utilities disconnected in the house. My aunt spoke to my mother, insisting that we take all of our things and leave. My mom stated, "We have absolutely no where to go, will you please give us thirty days and you may have the house. Please give us the time it takes to find a new home and process the appropriate documents." In the interim, my aunt took more action to set us up. My aunt continued to threaten our family and treated us as complete strangers with no desire to do us any good. My parents said, "Enough is enough, It was not worth it!" Rather than allow us additional time to find another space, my aunt decided to make false accusations and file claims against us in court.

The Word of God says, "I would not have you ignorant of the devil's devices." The Word also tells us that Holy Spirit will show us things to come. The Holy Spirit will warn you of the very thing that will happen in a person's life. The Holy Spirit showed me what was getting ready to happen to my family.

While all of the heartbreaking, careless acts continued, I had a dream. The Lord showed me that a whirlwind hit our home and we were forced out into the streets. The next day, I explained that dream to my mom, immediately, my mom prayed unto God, and He gave her the interpretation of that dream. My parents knew how God ministered to me in my dreams even at a very young age.

My parents decided to take action immediately. In haste, they began to move our belongings to a safer place, because we knew bad news was coming to our doorsteps.

Around 4:30 am the day after the dream, a hard knock was at the front door, a repeated knock I will never forget. My dad went to the door. There was a Sheriff Officer and in his hands was an Ex parte order that stated that we had to leave the premises immediately. We had to leave at 4:30 in the morning. We were homeless. We had to go to a relative's house. As my parents read the Ex parte order, their hearts were broken into pieces. That order was full of devastating false accusations. My aunt wrongfully accused us of abusing my grandmother! She knew this was the only way of having us removed in less than thirty days. What a journey it would be to put all the pieces of their hearts back together again.

My parents had to hire a lawyer to clear their names. In addition, my aunt pulled clothes out of the drawers then trashed the house to make it look like we were not good house keepers. She took pictures, presented them to the judge. My aunt stated to the Judge, "That was the condition in which they left the house." We were devastated! We gave up our very own home to take care of my dad's mother. Only to be falsely accused of abuse and now the bogus pictures? How could anyone do that to a family member? We were truly fine and content in our own home.

My parents' attorney asked the judge to allow us to get the rest of our belongings out of that house. The judge agreed. My aunt told the judge that we could come around her scheduled time, 5:30 pm that same day. This happened in the fall. At this time of the year, it gets dark earlier in the day.

We were most certainly at a disadvantage because of the time frame for moving. My aunt and the sheriff were scheduled to be there at that time and refused to allow any of my other family members to assist us with moving. So my dad, my mom, my younger brothers and myself had to move all of our things by ourselves. We lost so many precious things; so many memories were buried under debris. My aunt wanted us to suffer. We struggled to remove everything in the time allotted. Many things were left behind. My heart was broken in half. How can one move forward broken? As we moved our things, my aunt ridiculed and shamed us from one extent to the next. Complete humiliation from an aunt, a family member, as she stood outside laughing at us and making loud negative outbursts against my family.

It was so embarrassing to have my clothes in the street. Everyone in the neighborhood stood watching. As tears bubbled up in my eyes and the world started spinning around me, the sweet confident voice from my mother resounded in my ears. She said, "Don't cry, and hold your head up high; We will receive double for our shame! We will make it!" As soon as my mother said that, it was as if God Himself kissed me on my cheek. Hope ignited on the inside of me. Although it took time to find another place to call our own, her words meant so much to me. My mother's voice anchored me in the midst of our storm. Having her encouraging voice through our storms of life got us through to the other side.

We began our journey from homeless to HOPEFULNESS. Our homelessness was only for a short season. One thing I learned and will never forget is that family is where the heart is. A strong mother's faith in God will keep you while a daughter learns to stand on her own. Who is willing to believe God, that His best for your life is yet to come? Homelessness to hopefulness was truly a journey to be remembered. My parents didn't want to be a burden on anyone so we moved into a hotel for six months, paid six hundred dollars a week, and we ate out every night. There were times I would get depressed, darkness attempted to cloud my mind, but the words of my mother's voice rang louder on the inside of me, above the darkness coming around me mentally. Her voice cheered me up.

We were homeless. We were without a home to call our own, but homelessness only had to be for a season. Thank God we had the Word of God in our lives that gave us the faith we needed to get us through. Even though we stayed at that hotel for six months, we stayed together as family and we loved each other with all of our hearts and kept God in the midst of us. In that same year, we started attending a new church. The Pastor was one of the most positive people I ever met. This pastor was born a visionary, he taught my family how to pray, to speak against negative situations with the Word of God, and to decree the will of God for our lives. The Bible says, "What we do not see is more real than what we see, what we see is temporal but what is not seen is eternal." We did not see our new home but we knew it existed.

It was a little strange at the beginning of following my pastor's instructions, but afterward, I began to study the Bible for myself and I understood that God created us all to prosper. No matter if you were born with a silver or plastic spoon in your mouth, prospering is the will of God. Healing is the will of God. God has called us victorious, He sees us as Champions in His Kingdom. He called us to championship status before we were created in our mother's womb. It is the will of God for you to maintain your championship status. He has called us blessed, empowered to prosper, healed, already made whole, and wealthy, entitled to His continuous benefits.

The Bible says, "Hope deferred makes the heart sick." Hope without the manifestation of what you continue to anticipate can cause a dampness to lie over the very thing you believed God for and you begin to become discouraged and miss out on what was meant to be yours. Our hope was not deferred. We continued to hope. We believed that we would have a home, and soon our anticipation was fulfilled. God gave us double for our shame; we moved in our new home. We had four beautiful bedrooms, a formal dinning room, a cozy fireplace, and a two-car garage. Everyone had their own room! The true blessing was that it was everything we prayed for and more. Our home was at the Marlton's in Upper Marlboro, Maryland.

Most of all, God wants you to enjoy life regardless of the circumstances and situations. 3 John 1:2 reads, "Beloved, I wish above all things that you prosper and be in health, even as your soul prosper." Not knowing God's will for your life can allow you to feel hopeless in difficult situations. However, once God's will for you is known, you can go on to be the champion that He created you to be.

Dear God,
I thank you that I am on the path to a greater destiny. I believe you have called me to prosper. You are my leader and my guide to all roads in life. I ask you to keep my family blessed, healthy, wealthy and wise. I pray for every homeless person today and ask you to keep them safe and provide all of their needs. I thank you that you will bless me with the resources to one day help them.
In Jesus' name I pray, AMEN.

Chapter 3
Unplug Yourself

Take time out, to take in, to take over.
– Dr. Mike Freeman

I think an essential component to being successful is giving yourself a break. A break helps your mind to focus and reflect on your progress. This chapter is about balancing your life. By the end of this chapter, you will know how to effectively go away for a season in order to be a better person.

After every war, the military engages in a debriefing conference. After a fight, there is time to heal. After a major accident, you are hospitalized then referred to physical therapy if needed. During such times, many will reflect on everything they have done so far. We all need time to heal, to cry, and to regroup. I believe between each fight and challenge, you should take time off to recalculate your journey. I love taking vacations and going to the spa to help me regroup and relax. Some people work nonstop without giving themselves a break. None of us can run a race for 24 hours straight without passing out. So why do we run ourselves nonstop? You may need to unplug the phone, the internet, toxic relationships, or unplug from your worrying thoughts so that you can enter a place called rest.

After reading this chapter, I challenge you to turn off your television and your cell phone for an hour and sit in a quiet room to just think and regroup. Put your feet up and congratulate yourself on all of your accomplishments. We must enjoy each stage of our development. We deserve it!

Many of us are so busy helping everyone else reach their goals that we don't take out the time to focus on ours. Let me say this: there is an exchange in helping others, with balance of course. You can not be the best when you are running on fumes. A car can only drive so far before it runs out of gas. You must refuel in order to be the best. Nothing is better than a person returning to work, fresh from a vacation. There is nothing like a recharged battery or a full tank of gas. I dare you to take time off just for you. You deserve it! Yes! You are a Champion.

Genesis 2:2 reads "And on the seventh day God ended his work which he had made; and he rested on the seventh day from all his work which he had made."

Use the following space to write down all of things you need to unplug from in order to get closer to your goals.

Things You Need to Unplug From

Chapter 4
Be the Best You That You Can Be

*If you focus on your goals at least 30 minutes a day;
In 10 years, you would have spent 54,750 hours of your life changing your destiny. In addition, if you were paid just $10 for every hour, you would be $547,500 richer...
- Kellie Thompson*

Have you ever heard of an investor? An investor is an individual who puts money into the growth of a project expecting a larger return later on in life. Investing is future based. To create the life you want, you must invest in yourself to be the best. Commit to yourself today and do whatever it takes to become the best you can be.

A champion boxer trains all year even though he may only fight about twice that year. He educates himself about his opponents as he builds his technical skills and confidence for each match. Likewise, you must spend the necessary time building your technical skills and confidence to be ready when opportunity comes

Education gives you the information and technical skills it takes to be the best in whatever career you choose. Learn as much as you can about the career before you begin. Before you get into the driver's seat, someone must teach you how to drive that car. When you go through the proper training, you will possibly save time and make fewer mistakes. Some people choose to teach themselves. However, you will find that it could have been easier if you had received the proper training from an expert in that field.

The Bible states in 2 Chronicles 1:12 "Wisdom and knowledge is granted unto thee; I will give thee riches, and wealth, and, honor such as none of the kings have had that have been before thee; neither shall there any after the have the like."

Wisdom with understanding gives you discernment to know what to do, when to do it, and how to do it; like you know your name. Wisdom also allows you to produce results continually.

Wisdom is the ability to make executive decisions with understanding.

Once I became a licensed cosmetologist, I started receiving information about advanced training classes. Although, I was interested in taking the classes, I would not attempt to attend, because I lacked the capital at the time. However, when I noticed some of my colleagues who had taken the advanced classes worked faster and displayed fabulous hairstyles, I decided to invest in myself to become empowered. I got a budget together for the training, and decided to attend regardless of the cost. Every chance I got, I found myself in a different training session receiving more valuable information each time. I was like a sponge – training to be a Champion.

I began to see a major difference in my hairstyles. I also began to see a significant difference in my profits. I noticed that I had begun to increase more and more after attending each training session. The additional education became one of the keys to my success in becoming a champion. Education unlocks the door to success and allows you to walk freely and effectively in your craft. Education does not always have to be formal, as in taking a class with a professional instructor. I am simply encouraging you to use the resources available to you to educate yourself. Be the best that you can be.

Let's use for an example the steps a football team takes when preparing for a game. One of the first things they do is watch video tapes of the opposing team. They study their strengths and weaknesses so that they can learn what it will take to beat them. Secondly, they gather information from the tapes to create their plan of attack, thus defeating them by taking an advantage of their weaknesses.

Keep in mind that the opposing team is using the same strategy to prepare for the game, so you must know your own strengths and weaknesses so that you can work to sharpen your strengths and improve the areas you consider as your weaknesses. In life as a Christian, your opponent is Satan. His assignment is to steal, kill, and destroy. Therefore, we must continue to consider our weapon of defense which is our praise. Our praise weakens Satan's impact on our lives.

Psalm 68:1 reads "Let God arise, let his enemies be scattered" so when we worship God, it's like giving Satan a black eye. So we must worship God because it is our strength and Satan hates our worship. Yes! You are a Champion.

Because I have never entered a new facet of my career without researching first, I was able to achieve much more success than failure. I highly recommend anyone thinking about pursuing a career to do your research first. Going into any venture unprepared, uneducated, or uniformed will undoubtedly lead to your failure rather than success.

Research your career before entering instead of just jumping in blindly. This includes but is not limited to, going to the library or bookstore and getting all the resources available concerning your career. Before you invest in any business venture or career endeavor, research the pros and the cons to see if this is the correct path for you to take and how it will affect each part of your life. You are almost certain to be a champion in your field if you research it properly and follow the guidelines associated with your career choice.

PLAN! PRACTICE! PERSIST!

Creating a plan with persistence and practice will catapult you into a position of confidence. When you know your stuff, your confidence goes to a completely new level. Confidence is the ability to know who you are and what to do. Confidence is the absence of doubt and the presence of faith. Having all of these, you can't fail.

THE POWER OF RELATIONSHIPS

Another great resource for your education is going to come from observing your mentor. God has put mentors in my life who have helped me to be where I am today – happy and successful. I thank God for placing them in my life to help me. Their input in my life is a core ingredient to the success I am now experiencing. They helped me to make tough decisions that I could not make on my own. You must have someone in whom you can trust and with whom you can share your flaws and weaknesses so he or she can direct you to the best solutions for change. That person can lead you to principles of faith and persistence that will lead to increase in your life.

Even as a hairstylist, I was in search for a mentor. One day I was looking through some magazines and stumbled on a stylist by the name of Sherrita Matthews. Her work was outstanding and everything I wanted to produce was in that one photo. I saw style, sophistication, and timelessness. I had to meet the person who created the style from the photo. About 5 years later, I had the distinct honor to finally meet her when she started attending my church. You see God is always on time! To my surprise, she began styling at the salon where I was working. I would watch her for hours at a time and drill her with questions. And ever since, she has been in my life leading and guiding me into greater levels and depths in the hair industry. She has been such a wonderful inspiration in my career as well as my spiritual growth.

Positive relationships also help you get through the hard times. Mentors are always good to have around during times of hardship because they usually give you a sense of encouragement and hope, mostly because they have already experienced what you are going through and know that there is a way out. This is the part of education that you cannot buy anywhere.

My pastor, Dr. Michael Freeman, always says, "Hang with those who have your answers and get away from those who have your problem." He shares the importance of evaluating your inner circle. He teaches that you can see where a person is going based on their five closest friends. The people you hang out with are so very important to the direction of your growth and destiny. The only way I was able to escape poverty was by changing my environment and negative surroundings. You cannot hang around a Champion and remain a loser. Therefore, change your circle and you will change your future. You are a Champion. It's time to start hanging with them.

Chapter 5
Create Your Destiny

Active confessions create positive directions.
– Kellie Thompson

We were born to emulate God. He created the Earth with the words of his mouth. Like God, it is our destiny to create and it is our inheritance to create. If you are unsure of what your destiny is, take notice of what you think about day and night, as that is usually a clue to what you are destined to do. You create your destiny by the meditations of your heart. Meditation is your mental boot camp during your reading and thinking time. Read God's word and meditate on His promises found in the Bible. Once you think about something long enough, it begins to enter your heart. Once it enters your heart, it begins to grow and produce concepts and ideas. It begins to affect your thought process and influences your actions when you are faced with challenges. For example, research shows that after long-term negative self-talk, the body starts to deteriorate. Therefore, it is very important to use positive words and affirmations about yourself for healing to take place.

Many years ago, I started having meditation sessions. A meditation session is when you turn everything off but your brain and are without the interference of television, music, emails, and cell phones. You are only allowed to read scriptures and look at images in magazines to stimulate powerful thinking strategies. Pictures stimulate the brain, causing images to create feelings of possibilities. Meditation sessions are like one-on-one counseling sessions with God Almighty. But, if you don't take the time to pray and to meditate on God's word, meditation is empty. What directs you is your heart. What you put in your heart will come out whether you like it or not.

- *Where do you go to be a Champion?*
- *Who teaches you how to strive?*
- *Who inspires you to continue when your back is against the wall?*
- *How can we find hope in this world?*
- *To whom do you turn when the career you chose leads you to a closed door?*
- *What do you do next?*

We go to God. God created us as Champions. The Bible states in Genesis 1:26 "God created us in his image and in his likeness". You may ask, "Does this make us like God?" Well, yes. He said He made us in His likeness. Moreover, God is the greatest Champion of all times. Let God become your boxing coach when your back is up against the ropes. He will give you hope and the strength you need in troubled times. God is in your corner. God motivated me to not accept anything less than His best, even in troubled times. I was a little nervous in high school to ask the work study teacher if I could start my own business, but being a child of God, I had no reason to fear. I could not accept fear because fear is not of God. I asked the teacher. He granted my request, only under the promise that I followed through.

VISION CASTING EXERCISE

Habakkuk 2:2 "And the Lord answered me, and said, Write the vision, and make it plain upon tables, that he may run that readeth it. For the vision is yet for an appointed time, but at the end it shall speak, and not lie: though it tarry, wait for it; because it will surely come, it will not tarry."

The purpose of this exercise is to create a vision of how your life could possibly change for the better. A vision cast is a forecast of things to come in your future that you will declare to happen. For this exercise, you will need a poster board or a free wall in your house on which you can post your future goals. Next, you will need to get some magazines, and cut out some images that you wish to have in the future. I encourage you to buy some magazines you would not normally purchase. It may require that you venture beyond the magazine racks near the checkout counter at your local grocery store. Then paste the images up on your poster board or wall. The objective is to visualize your future by focusing on the pictures in front of you. Once you have completed your vision casting, you then will meditate on the images you posted as often as possible. Feel free, to make your vision cast as big and detailed as possible. If you wish, you can give yourself a time and date on your posted goals. I recommend placing a picture of yourself in the middle so you can see yourself in the middle of all of your future goals. You can cut out pictures of houses, cars, even photos of couples holding hands. If you have a study in your home, you can place it there to meditate on it. Some people use their refrigerator door to post future goals. I also recommend finding positive quotes and confessions to place on the poster board or wall.

Active confessions create positive directions. You are a Champion who will do whatever it takes to see your dreams fulfilled. With clear understanding of your goals, you will accomplish them faster because you have placed them in front of you.

If the weatherman's forecast calls for rain, will you pack your sunshade and beach ball? If you wish to become a doctor would you go to the police academy? So it is with your vision; each decision links to the next decision. If you want to become a doctor, maybe you can post the medical school of your choice. Place a picture of everything that it will take to accomplish your goals on your poster board, whether that be a person, place or a thing. It is your job to physically connect with each picture and idea you have posted to your vision cast. You want to make sure you have a clear understanding of what you really want to do before you start your process. I think it would be great to have a positive quote or a scripture of purpose to read and confess daily. For example, Isaiah 54:17, "no weapon formed against [my family] shall prosper" can be a scripture to confess over a picture of your family.

After changing the crowd of people with whom I associated, I began going to developmental sites.

THE POWER OF VISION CASTING

After changing the crowd of people with whom I associated, I began going to developmental sites, bringing back copies of floor plans and placing them on my refrigerator door. When you begin to place in front of you pictures of things you desire, you are creating a vision cast. Every day, I meditated and spoke things related to the vision cast on my refrigerator. I would get on the bus and walk through upscale neighborhoods to do what I referred to as stretching my mind, which means to expand your mental perception of what you deserve and what you can accomplish as a Champion. After months of meditating, I started meeting kids from the neighborhoods where I dreamed I would live. Before I knew it, I was invited into the same neighborhoods that I posted on my refrigerator. No longer did I just walk through to see the outside, but I was able to see the insides of the homes. Then I disconnected myself from the friends who were wasting their time smoking, drinking and using illegal substances. I started staying in school all day. My former friends said that I was "acting different". I wanted to act different. I wanted to live different. I wanted to dream different. You cannot keep doing the same things and expecting different results, so disconnect yourself from negative thinkers, speakers, and doers. Moreover, connect yourself with positive doers, speakers, and thinkers and Champions. You should start thinking like a Champion because You are a Champion!

Your lack of self -motivation is the only thing that can stop you in life.
– Kellie Thompson

Dear Heavenly Father,
I ask you to place people in my path that will help me and mold me into the person you created me to be. I ask you to remove the people whose intentions are not in my best interest. Give me the courage to walk away and never to regret my decision. From a distance,
let them see a change in me so that they will want to change their lives and be the best that they can be. I thank you God for wisdom and strength to be the best in every endeavor I choose because success is your will for me.
In Jesus' Name I pray, AMEN.

Chapter 6

Dare to be Different: Champions Are NOT Chameleons

The power of your self-image is equal to the fire that launches a space rocket. You can only elevate as high as your self-image
– Kellie Thompson

A chameleon is a tropical lizard of the family *Chamaeleonidae*, and is characterized by its ability to change color to blend in with its environment. If you are an inconsistent person, you are a champion and remember that! We should keep a constant flow of character. We should not try to adapt to every situation or environment. It is important to be diverse and to know how to act in different situations, you never change your identity. I can imagine it would be hard to be like everyone else and be happy within. I can imagine that it would get tiring after a while!

It is possible to be who you are and still be effective because you are an original. You do not have to copy what everyone else is doing to be successful. In the previous chapter, I talked about hanging around people you want to be like. I did not mean for you to become them and lose who you are as a person. You can follow their principles in your own skin.

In high school, I worked for a printing company whose responsibility was to help major companies go paperless. We transformed enormous amounts of their paperwork into digital files. I was working there in exchange for an hourly wage and high school credit for my senior year. I held several different positions there, ranging from the staple and paper clip remover to document scanner and data entry clerk. This type of work may seem demeaning, but it was nothing in comparison to the way the managers disrespected their employees. The managers were rude and cold, and had no problem disciplining the employees in front of others. In fact, my manager wrongfully terminated me in front of everyone just because he wanted me to work more than the twenty hours per week we had agreed to in order for me still to attend my other twelfth grade classes. You would think that my immediate reaction after being fired would be to get angry, sad, or worried; after all, I needed that job for high school credits so that I could graduate. But that is not what I did at all. I called my mother and told her that I was free.

...I am grateful that I experienced the hardship of being terminated from that job...

I decided to start a home-based business as a hair stylist. At first, I was afraid to start it because I did not know if my teacher would allow me to do something different from the requirement. Somehow, I was bold enough to ask the teacher if I started my own business could I still get credit for the class. He told me that if I created a business plan he would consider it.

After presenting him my business plan, he quickly agreed. He also required me to take pictures of my work and create comment sheets for my clients. I had to report back to him weekly. Looking back on the situation, I am grateful that I experienced the hardship of being terminated from that job because I possibly would have grown too comfortable with the company. If that manager had not been so mean, I probably would not have started my business so soon. After receiving that heavy blow, I could have been knocked out, but I survived that round. That became the moment that catapulted me into the successful business I enjoy today.

Your originality is a precious gift. During slavery, abolitionists dared to be different. Even at the risk of being alienated by society or killed, they fought against slavery and created freedom for the next generations. In doing so, they changed the lives of millions of Black Americans. As a result, they helped to empower blacks to have independence and self-respect. We must not enslave our minds to think we cannot use our originality to make a difference. We can all be champions and celebrate the difference in humanity. This can only happen when you dare to be different.

Remember God made us in his likeness. When God created you, there were no assembly lines. You are the hand-crafted original. Break any mold that does not line up with the Word of God. You are a Champion!

AUTHENTICITY TEST

What is on the inside of you that can change the dynamics of the world we live in? Are you the missing puzzle piece to cancer research? Will your ideas free a population of poverty? The following exercise is to help you develop your individuality. With the space provided create a list of things that make you original and give a suggestion how you can create increase for each item. For example, I am very creative; I used that trait to create my very own makeup line.

YOUR PRESENCE IS A PRESENT

Make your presence known. Your presence is a present to the world. Remember that and never forget it. God has a purpose for you. He created you with the imagination that could develop the cure for cancer. You possess the ability to help all the homeless people in your city. Never think you cannot make a difference. When you walk with integrity, self-respect and love, you will stand out to be different. It may take you some time but if you keep striving, it is possible. It is possible because you are a champion.

When I was a kid, we use to play this game called Truth or Dare. We use to sit in a circle and challenge one another to do different things.

LET US PLAY TRUTH OR DARE!

I dare you to dream big.
I dare you to strive harder.
I dare you to believe in the impossible.
I dare you to thank God every day.
I dare you to shout out "**I am a champion**".
I dare you to speak up for what you believe in.
I dare you to smile big.
I dare you to have integrity.
I dare you to break the cycle of ordinary.
I dare you to start a business.
I dare you to stop smoking.
I dare you to stop drinking.
I dare you to stop complaining and do something.
I dare you to live today without crying.
I dare you to practice extraordinary kindness to others.
I dare you to P.U.S.H. (Pray until Something Happens.)

Dear God,
I thank you for creating me a champion. I love who you made me to be. I thank you that I am a Champion in my own skin. I am the best me that I can be and when you made me you did not make any mistakes. Therefore, I again thank you for making me. In addition, I promise to walk with my head held high.
In Jesus' name I pray, AMEN.

Chapter 7
Never Silence Your Voice

Your words are keys to your destiny.
– Kellie Thompson

One of the most inspiring people I have ever read about was Mother Theresa. I would go to the book store and sit for hours and read her letters to those who followed her ministry. As I read them, I would visualize her speaking directly to me. Mother Theresa's voice touched nations by her love and charity. For 19 years, she taught at Saint Mary's high school in Calcutta. The suffering and poverty outside the convent walls made such a deep impression on her, that in 1948 she received permission from her superiors to leave the convent school and devote herself to working among the poorest of the poor in the slums of Calcutta.

Although she had no money, she started a school for less fortunate children. She founded *The Missionaries of Charity* whose primary task was to love and care for those who most likely would have been left behind. By the 1990's there were over one million co-laborers in more than 40 countries. Millions now try to follow Mother Theresa's spirit and charity in their families.

Mother Theresa died on September 5, 1997. While she lived on earth she never silenced her voice, but spoke up for what was right and noble. She believed every human being deserved freedom and civil rights. She led millions to freedom through faith and love. She gave freedom of the mind, the heart and the spirit to millions of people. She won a Nobel Peace prize in 1979. Yes! She was a Champion.

Your voice could be the next voice of peace and love to millions of people. Your voice has so much power, that it is like the fire that flows out of a space rocket. Use your fire to, catapult you into your success filled destiny. Use your voice to speak words of motivation to change the world around you, starting with the members in your family. Even the birds use their voice early in the morning! They wake us up with the songs of praise. You look outside and there they are on the trees singing.

> ***Never Silence your Voice... There is so much wealth in your voice...***

They have a purpose on this earth to use their voice to let us know that it is morning. The birds singing gives many people natural tranquility because it is not man made. It is not like traffic and police sirens; it is a pure sound of nature. It is something God has given to all of us to enjoy. Never silence your standards and contributions to mankind. There is so much wealth in your voice. No one has the right to tell you anything different. If someone tells you that your voice does not count, slap him or her up side their head and knock some sense in them. Ha! Ha! Ha! I am just kidding. Just don't believe them.

VOICE IN ACTION

A voice in action has the ability to determine if a man or woman will get married. I have attended many weddings in my lifetime. Each time, the preacher asked, "Does anyone object to this union?" I sometimes wondered why they did that. I thought about it one day, and my life was instantly changed. Why does the opinion of the guests matter? Moreover, what right do they have to object to the couple's decision?It's true, we have the power to stop a wedding - someone else's ceremony.

If you have that much power to object to a major decision of a couple getting married, why can't you speak up when it comes to your own decisions? Do not silence your voice.

Speak now or forever hold your peace.

Speak now or forever live in depression.

Speak now or forever be in debt and poverty.

Speak now or forever bury your dream.

Speak now or forever be a renter.

Speak now or forever lower your self-worth.

Speak now or forever be on government assistance.

Speak Now!

If you don't like what you are seeing in your life, stop it; change what you are speaking and hearing. The scripture said that "you can have whatsoever you say". By the word of your mouth you create your world.

I have chosen to speak positively over my life and now it is time for you to speak positively over yours. No longer will you be a negative statistic; today you shall become the Champion God intended for you to be. You will survive this round. Awaken the Champion on the inside of you and begin to declare your victory. You have the power; it's in your tongue. It's true.

USE YOUR VOICE

Life and death are in the power of the tongue (Proverbs 18:21). Watch carefully what you say. Give life to your vision by speaking it into existence and, stop killing your dreams by speaking negatively about your temporary and uncomfortable situation. **Your temporary situation is not your identity. You are a Champion.**

Through faith, everyday challenges can become lifelong victories. Speaking, as I stated in chapter one, is the first major action in meeting your goals. To meet your goals you must speak positive things over yourself. If you don't know what to say, say what the word of God says about you. You are more than conquerors!!!

I constantly meditate on God's word to give me strength during hardships. I also take the necessary steps to pursue the things that I have studied. I constantly use my voice to recite scriptures so that I can plant them in my heart. James 1:22 tells us, "To be not only be hearers of the word but to be doers also". Regardless of what obstacle comes, I continue to fight oppression like the Champion that I am. In addition, I always conquer my goals because I conquer my thoughts. Instead of speaking what I feel or hear, I speak what God himself has promised me concerning my situation.

I confess with my mouth and I believe in my heart that what I have spoken shall come to pass in the name of Jesus. After I make my confessions, I begin to thank God for the thing that I believe for until it manifests in my life.

I believe success comes from using your voice to plant seeds into your future. When you have a clear understanding of your goals, you are encouraged to pursue them. Dr. I. V. Hillard said, "Where there is clarity of vision, there is acceleration towards the goal." Your voice has the ability to accelerate your goals. Each word becomes a picture and each picture becomes a concept of possibility.

Your words are the keys to your victory, wealth and

freedom to your future.

Remember, in addition to being a destiny-speaking Champion, you must be a Champion of integrity. If you say you are going to do something, do it. If you are running late for a business meeting, call to say that you are going to be late. If you cannot make it, at least call to reschedule. Calling shows that you care and respect that person's time. That simple act makes you a champion with integrity. Integrity produces wealth, and trust. When you are a person of integrity, people will have more confidence in you. In fact when people have confidence in you, they will be more likely to refer others to you for goods, services, or promotions.

Remember the word of God says life and death is in the power of your tongue. The Word of God also says; your tongue is as a pen of a ready writer. Just as Mother Theresa wrote into the lives of millions by the words she spoke, you possess that same power to speak existence to your destiny.

Dear God,
I thank you for giving me a strong voice. I pray that I will use my voice to glorify you in everything I do. I ask you to create opportunities to use my voice to share your love to those in need. I will never under estimate the power of my voice or my words; because my words bring forth life. I will keep my voice and my words only for the positive and good that is found in the Bible.
I thank you for your wisdom on how to speak boldly without fear and I thank you that my voice is changing my world around me every day. I am determined to bring glory to you and to you alone.
In Jesus' name I pray, AMEN.

Chapter 8
Dreams Can Become Reality

To change your results, you must change your actions.
- Unknown

Have you ever had a dream that has not been fulfilled yet? Maybe you got distracted, discouraged or have just given up. Today, I encourage you to dream again. If you have been doing the same thing with nothing happening, you must change your plan of action in order to see your dream become your reality. "If you desire to see different results, you must change your actions. A dream consists of voluntary and involuntarily images, ideas, emotions and suggestions in your mind. In order for your dreams to be your reality, it is going to involve your images.

Dr. Martin Luther King had a dream that all of humanity would live in unity. His dream was real to him because it caused him to take action against civil injustice. He used his dream and his voice to lead a Civil Rights march in Washington, D.C. It was there that he shared his dream with the world. He spoke it as it was revealed to him. He lived out that dream in his mind repeatedly. He spoke life to a dead situation. He fought for equality for all nationalities. He shared his dream in the form of a speech and created change by using his voice to speak words of life and strength to millions. Today black men and white men are working together in unity. He fought the good fight of faith and persistence until his death in 1968. Although he is deceased, his dream and legacy is now our reality. He was a Champion! Though we continue to fight for unity for all humanity across the globe, Dr. Martin Luther King, Jr. was a visionary of unity. His life has inspired me to believe that dreams can become reality. His children are experiencing their father's dream for unity in America and around the world.

Proverbs 13:22 reads, "A good man leaves an inheritance for his children's children." What will you leave behind for your children's children? Will it be poverty? Will it be the will to win? Dr. Martin Luther King's dream became a reality through his courage to share his dream with the world. Sharing your dream is just as important.

I HAVE A DREAM

My dream is to train and motivate generations to use faith to conquer and possess the things that God has placed in their hearts. My dream of mentorship is now a reality. I have helped hundreds of young people through mentorship and positive word-seeds of faith. My biggest investment is imparting into the lives of others. I plan to help change the economic status of this generation and generations to come. I plan to continue my journey of influencing the lives of millions of young people across the globe, stretching their capacity for possibilities. Dr. King and Mother Theresa have demonstrated the possibilities that dreams can come true with education, constant discipline, and dedication. Although they were hit with heavy blows, they walked in victory as a Champion.

One night I had a vivid nightmare that a monster was chasing me. I cannot recall where I was, but I do remember I was being chased by something I could not recognize. A massive, dark being, larger than anything I had ever seen was after me. All I could do was run and it seemed as if I could not do anything to escape. I was sweating from running so hard and got to a point to where there was nowhere else to run. Then, just as suddenly as the chase ended, I woke up, grateful that it had not been a real-life situation. Everything had seemed so real. Although my body didn't move from the bed, my body had physically reacted to the horror I experienced during my sleep. The profuse perspiration from the nightmare had transcended into the natural world and soaked my bed sheets and I was even crying when I woke up.

I never came to a conclusion about the meaning of that nightmare, but I concluded that if something exists in your mind strongly enough, it will dictate your actions in the physical world. This works with positive thoughts as well. If you meditate on positive thoughts, your body will eventually react in a positive way. The thought will lead to emotion, and then an idea. Once you have an idea, you can produce an action.

If you meditate on positive thoughts, your body will eventually react in a positive way.

HOME OWNERSHIP IS A REALITY

Before I purchased my first home, I created a plan of action. I took a picture of the house where I wanted to live. I placed the picture of the house on my nightstand so that when I woke up, I would see where I was going to live soon. I often visited the neighborhood where the house was in order to increase my focus and my faith. I would sit in the car outside of the house and pray over it. Then, I would close my eyes and envision myself in the living room sipping on a cup of tea. Reciting my new address became a regular habit and I even practiced writing the address on the upper left corner of an envelope. I believed in my heart that it was my house. I joined my thoughts with my body and physically acted on my dream. I told my friends that I was moving soon. Moreover, I told them that I was going to have a barbeque in the summer.

Soon, my dream of homeownership had become a reality. Thirty days later, I moved in that house. It was amazing because the process of mental focus coupled with action helped me to purchase my home. It was also amazing to see the proud looks on the faces of my friends at the barbeque the next summer. My dreams are not the only dreams that can become reality. If my dream of home ownership happened for me, it can also happen for you. Follow the processes discussed in this book because every process in here actually worked. It may take a little time, but when you have faith and patience, you will see your dreams in full manifestation no matter how big your goals may seem.

Follow your dream with the appropriate plan of action...

Understand that saving for the purchase of my home did not come easily. I had to make some wise decisions. I refrained from frequent shopping sprees (not an easy thing for me) and I practiced discipline in my finances. My daily morning latte had to become a random treat because I knew I had a bigger picture in mind. I had to save money and stick to my budget. I still went out from time to time, but I kept my goal in perspective.

If you dream to own a house, keep dreaming and you will have it if you follow your dream with appropriate action. You may have some outstanding debt that you need to pay off to attain that dream. If you have more than three credit cards, try minimizing them by half to improve on your credit score. Why not start saving for a down payment and closing cost for your dream home? This will show that you are serious about getting your dream home. Start doing things like shopping around to find the lowest interest rate and when the time comes, negotiate the lowest interest rate possible. The lower the rate, the lower your monthly payments will be. In doing so, you can save money to reach your goals.

IT'S TIME TO START THAT BUSINESS

If you have a dream to start a small business, create a business plan. You can buy information on how to create a business plan at your local bookstore. Before you answer the upcoming questions, get a pen and paper to write your answers down. These questions should give you an idea of how to start your business plan. Your answers to the questions below will make your dream more clear and push you in the right direction. A clear dream will keep you motivated to continue and you will be more productive. I am not referring to just seeing more clearly, but also to making sure your heart is in the right place. If you believe you are destined for greatness, “Mental Toughness for Success” by Dr. I.V. Hilliard is a must read. This book changed my life both spiritually and naturally. Dr. I.V Hilliard says, “When my heart is right towards God, He is obligated to orchestrate the circumstances, the events and situations of my life to bring me into the knowledge of the things I need to know and people I need to know that are critical for the fulfillment of my purpose and destiny in life." Isn't that awesome?

Now take some time to carefully answer the questions that follow:

- *Do you know what area in which you want your business to be located?*
- *How will your business help the next generation?*
- *How will your educational background help your business?*
- *How much money do you hope to make?*
- *Can you start your business in your home?*
- *Do you plan to buy or lease a building?*
- *Do you want to have a business partner?*
- *Have you dreamed to start your business in your country or internationally?*

Although it is easy for many to start a business, often times it is difficult to continue due to lack of understanding and lack of an air-tight business plan. I recommend you read over your business plan as often as possible. This process will encourage you to continue even through difficult times. All the work will pay off and you will be able to leave that stressful job you are in before you know it.

Keep a positive opinion of yourself. How you view yourself is the code of standard that determines what you will/ will not allow yourself to do. When your self-image is positive, those you serve in business will view you as a well-decorated gift with the big bow on top and your business will be a greater success. With negative self image, you will look and feel like an unwrapped gift. It looks as though there was no thought put into giving it. Who wants that? Remember dreams can become reality. The only thing that exists between your dreams and your reality is time. What you do with that space of time will determine whether you reach your dreams or not. So get started and stand in faith to see your dreams come true. In the meantime, you must act as if your dreams have already come true by faith. You must act like a Champion, think like a Champion, because you are a Champion.

Dear God,
Thank for this wonderful day. Thank you that I am breathing and I have eyes to see the vision and purpose you have placed in me. Thank you for the grace and favor that you have placed in my life. I surrender my dreams to you. Thank you for the ability to see my dreams come true. I believe that dreams can become a reality because of you. I can do the impossible because of you. You have already given me the strength and wisdom to fulfill each phase. I ask you the give me more and more dreams and the resources needed to accomplish them. I ask you to send the people in my path to help make this a reality. I ask you for handpicked customers that will love and appreciate my business concept and services. I ask you God for the wisdom to help someone else in need once my dreams are manifested.
In Jesus' name I pray, AMEN.

Chapter 9
Get Back Up

Just because you fell down does not mean you have to stay down.
– Kellie Thompson

You must exercise positive mental strategies everyday to win the battle over challenges that seem to keep you from getting back up. This can be as simple as saying to yourself, "I can do it," even if you do not believe it at first. Whether you realize it or not, you will conform to whatever you say the most. Therefore, if you practice positive mental strategies, you can survive extreme mental pressures from everyday struggles and obstacles. You must work hard and train hard to be a Champion. An example of this process is in the sport of boxing. After being knocked down during a boxing match, you have 10 seconds to get up and continue to fight. The boxer who has just been knocked down by lifes challenges must decide either to stay down or to get up. He can take the easy way out and just stay down and lose the fight or he can get up, fight some more and possibly win. One thing is for sure: his chance of winning is 0% if he stays down. You may feel victimized but please get back up! Child of God I know it was a low blow and you did not see it coming, but get up. You have to get up!

They may have cheated or falsely accused you to discredit your character, but you must hold on! Do not let them get you down or keep you down. Rise to the occasion and claim your victory. Know that your vision will come to pass if you faint not. Galatians 6:9 reads "And let us not be weary in well doing: for in due season we shall reap, if we faint not" Until then, stay positive, continue your journey, and keep fighting. You can do it, because you are a CHAMPION!

I encourage you to get back up, no matter how long you have been down. As long as you have God in your corner and the will to fight, winning is within your reach. Even if people are yelling for you to throw in the towel, just ignore them and claim your victory. Claim your victory now, because you are a champion!

As long as you have God in your corner and the will to fight,winning is within your reach...

My mother gave birth to me in the same year she graduated from high school. Many gave their opinions of what she should do with her life because it looked as though she had ruined it, but she was determined to succeed. Throughout my childhood, she lived on public assistance and worked small jobs. Nevertheless, she would say, "I am going to college and we are not going to live this way forever". She always told me to never despise small beginnings because destiny is greater than what we know. I always kept that in my mind and I still do to this day. Now, my mom has an undergraduate degree in Computer Information Systems and a Masters in Education. She never let anything hold her back. She also started a business in year 1996, and now owns a Learning Center and helps children with special needs. She is the founder of the *Not My Kids Foundation,* a non-profit organization for at-risk youth in urban neighborhoods. She was the first example in my life that proved that it is not how you start the race but how you finish the race that matters. When most people would have considered having a child immediately after graduating from high school a "knock-out" punch, my mother seemed to use the situation as encouragement to do even better for herself and for me. Giving up was not an option as she had more than herself in mind.

VICTORY OVER DEBT

"Our challenges are only as big as we perceive them to be"

In 2005, I was in over my head with bills and I was sitting in my office looking over all the bills and debt that I had accumulated. I was worrying so much that I started losing my hair. Then I started praying. Hallelujah! God told me exactly what to do. So I placed all of my bills on the floor, and laid down on top of them, and had my husband pray with me. Then after we prayed, God told me to get up and to physically stand on top of those bills. I felt so good. There I was, standing on top of a mountain of bills and with the victory of knowing I had already conquered them in my mind. They were paid in full at that point. The natural world just needed to catch up. This action was a positive mental strategy that symbolized my victory over debt. In addition, I started calling myself the **Debt Terminator** and I went to war. I started paying off debt left and right and in one month, I had paid off almost a thousand dollars worth of debt. In addition, every day I said aloud "I am debt free" until it manifested in my life.

> *...If God be for me, then who can be against me? You can win this round child of God...*

Do not let debt beat you; you beat it because you are a Champion. Debt can only be as big as you make it. If you allow it to become a monster, it will be one, but if you would just change your thinking and begin to worship God, he then becomes magnified and no monster or demon in hell is big enough to fight against the God in you! For the Bible says in Romans 8:31, "If God be for me, who can stand against me?" You can win this round child of God. Therefore, even if it appears to be the end of the fight, you still have more rounds to go. Get up and stay in the fight because you are a Champion.

STAY UP

Now that the importance of getting up is clear, you must understand that staying up is just as critical. Erect your thinking and make up in your mind, in your heart and in your spirit to stay up. Even if the tears are flowing down your cheeks, do not allow your emotions to trick you. Keep your mind on what really matters. Victory! Your emotions can be your worst enemy sometimes because if you feel defeated most likely you will want to give up. You cannot. You may even ask if the fight is over. If you have not reached your goal, the answer is no. Keep your hands up and keep focusing on God and his promises and you will win. You will win because You are a Champion!

Struggles may seem to be getting the best of you right now, but you cannot give up. It was a struggle for me to see my self-value while I was homeless, but that did not matter because my reflection was on God. I had to stay up. I would say to myself "this is temporary. I am hopeful, I will have a home very soon, and I am a Champion". I would sing songs of praise. I would thank God daily for healing me from my present condition. I decided I was going to stay up. So I stayed up in my word,

I stayed up in my thinking and I stayed up in my actions. It's amazing, I really had to trust God every step of the way. It is easy for others to tell you to trust God, but difficult situations will teach you that God is truly your source. Will you trust him?

Write down a situation that has happened in the past that had knocked you down or think of a time you have given up. Now recreate that situation, only this time with the information you have learned. How would you handle the situation now?

Dear God,
I thank you for the strength to get back up. I pray that I will never let anything hold me down again. I have the ability to stay in the fight until I win. I bind doubt, low self-esteem and fear and I loose courage, strength and endurance. I also thank you for sending people in my path to help me fight and encourage me to victory. I am debt free and I always win.
In Jesus' name I pray, AMEN.

Chapter 10
You are Important

Have you ever been walking in the middle of the night, and hit your toe on something? Although you just hit your toe, it probably felt like your entire foot was in pain. Whether you are a superstar or a worker at Starbucks, a janitor or the CEO of a janitorial service, you are important to God. Is the toe less important than the entire foot? Just as the human body needs every part, so does this world need you.

THE MARVELLOUS YOU

YOU are important to God and to this world. When YOU were born, heaven smiled. The earth rejoiced at the wonderful gift that YOU are. Walk with your head held high because YOU are a Champion. Although you were born into an uncertain world full of doubt and fear, when YOU were born, something changed. Something stopped and hope began to grow. Do you know how important YOU are to this world? Do you know that YOU can change the conditions of your house, the conditions of your neighborhood, or even the conditions of this nation? Maybe YOU are reading this and saying, "She can't be talking about me? That may be true for someone else, but not me." I am talking about YOU. I am talking directly to YOU! YOU are a Champion. YOU will win this round. The very fact that God Himself made YOU is the proof that YOU are important. He fashioned YOU to be something special with a big bow on top. God took his time to make all of us. I am talking about the same God who made the heaven and the earth; He made YOU.

Psalms 139:14 says, "YOU are fearfully and wonderfully made and one of His marvellous works." Stop reading for a second, go look in the mirror and tell yourself, "I love me and no matter what, I am going to walk in victory. I am a marvellous champion".

Never forget the power you have within yourself. God has a purpose for your life. The same creative power that God used to create the world resides on the inside of you now. Never doubt yourself or the promises found in the word of God. Always have faith in yourself, dream the impossible, and strive for excellence in all that you do. You are not a second-class citizen, so do not allow anyone to tell you differently. If you have already accepted Christ as your Lord and Savior, you were reborn into royalty. You are important. You are on top in every area of life because you are a child of God. Romans 8:16-17 reads, " The Spirit itself beareth witness with our spirit, that we are children of God: And if children, then heirs; heirs of God, and joint-heirs with Christ; if so be that we suffer with him, that we be glorified together."

...Never forget the power you have within yourself...

One day someone asked me what my name meant and I told them it means "Elite." No, I never read that in a book but that is what it means to me. I have the power to create with the words of my mouth. Therefore, every time I hear my name, I think "elite". Every time I see my name on paper, I see elite. In my mind, I see myself as a heir of God and a joint-heir with Christ in the elite army of God. The only book I allow to tell me my true reflection is the Bible. That is the greatest book to read if you want to define yourself. No one but God can define your essence, because He is the one who made you. Therefore, the next time a negative speaker tries to give you the definition of your essence, shut them up and say, "Who are you to define me? God made me a CHAMPION."

THE ESSENCE OF ME

The following exercise is designed to locate the way you view yourself. Answer each question with the spaces below

I am important to

____

____

____

____

____

When I look in the mirror I see

____

____

____

____

____

When people are around me they feel

____

____

____

____

____

When I leave the earth, I want to be remembered as

____

____

____

____

____

Dear God,
Thank you for creating me a champion. Grant me the wisdom and insight of how to use the strength I have within myself. God, you have a purpose for my life and I shall walk in it daily. I understand that the same creative power that God used to create the world resides on the inside of me now. Forgive me for ever doubting myself and I declare that I will stand on the promises found in the word of God forever. I will strive for excellence in all that I do. I accept Christ as my Lord and Savior. I am important in you. And I live on top in every area of my life because I am child of God.
In Jesus name, AMEN.

Chapter 11
Keep the Flame Burning

The Olympics were derived from the ancient Greeks. They consider fire to be the divine element of the games. They would place a perpetual fire in front of their principle temples and they would use the sun and a special mirror to light the torch. Today the flames are lit using the same technique to preserve its authenticity. After the flame is lit, a torchbearer runs a lap around the stadium before the flame is used to light the Olympic cauldron. It remains lit for the duration of the games. At the end of the closing ceremony, the fire is put out, but reignited every year before the Olympic Games begin. Although the flames are physically extinguished, the symbol and pride for the sport never goes out.

Fire is a natural element. I believe that fire is a divine sign of unity and strength. Fire is universal and used in every element of society. It is used to change physical properties. Fire burns, cleans, melts, ignites, warms, and lights a room. Fire is also used to purify gold and silver. Fire is powerful, and if used properly, it is very effective. Moreover, if fire is used improperly it can be destructive.

Each year, the Olympics introduce new athletes to the games. Each athlete may be somewhat nervous but still confident because they know they have trained. Former Olympians not only passed the torch, but also the legacy and tradition of the Ancient Greeks. This concept can easily apply to our everyday lives. Think of it this way; every day Champions are born into the body of Christ and we are responsible to pass the torch. It is our responsibility to prepare the way for them to become champions as well. Go out and pass the flame of commitment to the next generation.

Matthew 11:10 reads, "For this is he, of whom it is written, Behold, I send my messenger before thy face, which shall prepare the way before thee." That applies to you too.

Just as John the Baptist was sent to prepare the way of Jesus, our assignment is to prepare the way for generations to come. When I pass my torch, I want it to be fully lit and burning brighter than ever. That torch will represent my vibrant legacy that allows the one behind me to start from where I left off. Glory to God! Do you want to pass a torch with a low burning flame or worse, a flame that is completely extinguished? We all leave a legacy behind believe it or not. Let us make a promise to pass a torch with excellence and integrity. A flame full of wisdom and strength. A flame that will always represent "Champion".

> *We all leave a legacy behind believe it or not. Let us make a promise to yourselves to pass it with excellence and integrity...*

Say this "I will leave a fully ignited torch; I will pass a torch of wisdom and strength to my next Generations."

After reading this book, I pray that a lasting flame has developed in your heart to share it with **someone else**. Will you lead the next generation to victory? As stated in a previous chapter, Mother Theresa helped thousands of people around the world. Will you learn from her example and do something to influence the world around you? As I began to read Mother Theresa's letters and quotes about helping others, a fire began to burn in my heart. The spirit of love ignited my heart and filled it with great compassion. Her extraordinary kindness and selfless commitment in serving others has inspired me to do the same. True compassion caused my mom and I to start our foundation for at risk youth. We are now a part of a great movement that is taking place in the lives of young people in urban communities. Moreover, we are experiencing an overwhelming fire that will never go out. Yes! We are Champions.

FINAL EXAM

I encourage you to become a leader in your community on purpose. Join a local recreational center to impart wisdom and courage into our young people. Share love to make the world a better place to live and dream. Make a commitment to make the best out of your life; every single moment. Stay optimistic through it all. Keep faith active in your life. Faith is the fuel to your flame. Faith helps you to see the goal and not the present situation. Help someone in need, starting with those in your household and family. Do not just walk past without at least sharing eye contact and a smile. Help someone who needs the help. They may not need money; they may just need your strength and your ignited flame to recharge.

Faith is the fuel to your flame. Faith helps you to see the goal and not the present situation...

Now that you have read the principles in this book and started your journey for personal development, help someone else. Make it a practice to say thank you to those who took time to help you in every phase of your journey. Write them a letter or send them a card. Remember to take time and celebrate your victories in each stage of completion. Live for purpose every day. Make it a goal to increase daily. Keep faith as your core value. You have everything you need right now to win. You can truly turn everyday challenges into victory through faith. Finally, remember to keep God first. It is only in Him that you are truly a winner. Yes! You are a CHAMPION!

Dear God,
I thank you for this beautiful day. Thank you for the gift of a new season. Father, I thank you I will walk free in your purpose for my life. I will win in every area of my life, I dedicate my life to you. Use me Lord daily. Bless me with the eyes of you, so that I may see things your way. I ask you for the heart and compassion of Jesus, so that miracles can take place in my life. I ask for the wisdom of the Holy Spirit. So that I may have insight and foresight of your will for my life. I ask you to reveal and expose the things that are not pleasing in your sight. Renew me again. Cleanse my heart from all dead works. I thank you God for a clean slate. Glory to your name. Holy, holy, holy and perfect are you God in all of your ways. I surrender all to you and I submit my will to you this day and forever more!
In Jesus' name I pray, AMEN.

Prayer of Salvation

Romans 10:9-10 States, "That if you confess with thy mouth the lord Jesus and believe in your heart that he is raised from the dead you shall be saved. For with the heart man believed unto righteousness and the mouth confession is made unto salvation."

Say this prayer aloud...

'Jesus I believe that you died and rose from the dead on my behalf as my eternal sacrifice. I repent of all my sins and ask that you forgive me and cleanse me of all unrighteousness. I ask that you come into my heart and abide in me. I make you Lord of my life and I thank you for saving me now.

Congratulations, you are now in the family of God.

About This Book...

"Positive confessions create positive directions"

GOD created us Champions. He created us to win. It is our destiny to win and our birthright to win. He anointed you with the ability to turn everyday challenges into victory. Do not ever be afraid to go after your dreams. Before you were born, God equipped you with everything you need to live in victory. This book will help you to walk as a champion in every area of life. This book will serve as your mental boot camp. Your thinking will be stretched and sharpened as you read and do the exercises found in this book.

Kellie shares practical word of wisdom and principles that changed her destiny from homelessness to a six figure income by twenty-five years old. She explains how understanding the power of your mental state will accelerate your physical state. She teaches you how life challenges are only as big as you perceive them to be. She coaches you to a better and brighter future.

About This Author...

Meet Kellie Thompson, she is a native of Washington, DC. She has been a licensed cosmetologist since 2000, master stylist for 6 years, and certified make-up artist for 9 years. She is the owner of *Successful Looks, LLC*, a premier leader in the hair care and cosmetic industry. We want to help every woman enhance her natural beauty by providing the finest hypo-allergenic products. These products are infused with natural minerals, oils, and Vitamins A, C, and E. It's no surprise that *Successful Looks* has established quite a buzz in the hair care and cosmetic industry.

Founded in April 2010, hair and skin-care are the company's focus - everything *Successful Looks* uses is hypo-allergenic and organic. The company, too, has grown organically. In the past, Kellie used other product lines and saw immediate break-outs, chemical burns from relaxers, and long-term hair breakage. After years of the issues, she began to use organic hair care products, often mixing them to make products even gentler for her clients. Ultimately, Kellie knew she had to develop her own hair care system. With the help of experienced chemists, Kellie also launched her hypo allergenic, organic make-up line.

Kellie has travelled the country as a beauty professional and platform artist. She has worked with the renowned *Dudley Product Company* and *Elasta QP*. Her work has been featured in national magazines such as *Hype Hair, Style Q* and featured on the cover of *Black Hair* as the "#1 Hairstyle of 2007". She is a two-time winner of *The Golden Scissor Award*, which was featured on the public television channel, *PBS*.

This catapulted her into other television appearances such as the reality show *Textures and Tones* on *TV One*, and the local morning news on FOX 5. Kellie's exposure is not limited to the screen, but she has graced the airwaves as well via various local and national radio stations such as *Heaven 1580, WHUR 96.3* and various other *Radio One* stations. She works with hundreds of children in her local community by volunteering as a Sunday School teacher. She is President and CEO of *SuccessLooks.com*, a business that empowers women to become fashion jewelry consultants to earn extra income for their families. And after three years of being a *M.A.C.* professional, she recently launched her cosmetic line, *Successful Looks Product, Inc.* (SPI). Kellie has a 3 year Certificate in Biblical Studies from *Spirit of Faith Bible Institute* and is an active leader in youth ministry. She is the Vice President of *Not My Kids Foundation*, a non-profit organization that focuses on at-risk, inner-city youth. She has spoken to hundreds of children, sharing her life experiences as a source of hope in an uncertain world. She is a leader and mentor to many and her life has inspired many and she has vowed to continue to fight for her generation and the generations to come.

Acknowledgements

First I would like to give all Honor and Glory to God who without him no of this would be possible. To my husband, my heart and first love Marty Thompson who held things together while I invest hours and hours into this project and helped make this happen. To my parents William and Patrina Suydam who are my support system and always being there for me and teaching how to walk out my destiny. My Brothers William, Matt who I honor and cherish for always keeping me in line and supporting me in everything I do. To my Grandmother who is my power source who I can always depend. To my cousin Sharone Makins who was the first person who helped me on this project and spoke life into this project. To my mentors Debbie Grant and Cynthia Washington, these two women have guided me through the last five years of my life helping me to see the possibilities. To my family who has supported me and keep me focused on my dreams and because you them I am who I am today. To my best friends Deitra, Jada ,Keisha, and Natalie thanks for your hours of advice you have giving to me, you guys have ALWAYS been there. To my friends Jennifer, Brelyn, Carla, Tori, Jessica and Lakeisha thanks for your push and prayers that help me to complete this project. And so many others who are connected to my destiny. To my Pastors Mike and Dee Dee Freeman my spiritual parents who I love so very much. To Danita

Brooks my dear friend and editor who spent countless hours on making this project a success. To Troy and Kelley Woods for my look on my cover. I would like to thank Ridgley Makins for your priceless hours of motivation and dedication to assist me in so many ways, love ya tons. Special thanks all of my publication partners Stephanie Thomas, Geraldine Makins, Marion Makins, Carla Lee, Jennifer Lucy, Roscoe Holley, Yvonne Robinson, Patrina Suydam, Mary Coles, Lakeisha Jacobs, Tiffianne Hudnall, Genneen Harrington, William Suydam Sr